Javaad Alipoor
co-created with Kirsty Housley

Rich Kids

A History of Shopping Malls in Tehran

Salamander Street

PLAYS

First published in 2022 by Salamander Street Ltd.
(info@salamanderstreet.com)

ISBN: 9781913630515

10 9 8 7 6 5 4 3 2 1

The Javaad Alipoor Company previewed *Rich Kids* at Theatre in the Mill (Bradford) in July 2019 before opening at The Traverse as part of their Edinburgh Festival programme. The show then transferred to HOME Manchester for a two week run in October 2019. A subsequent UK tour in early 2020 was cancelled due to the COVID19 pandemic.

Unable to perform the show live, and with continued support from Battersea Arts Centre, Norfolk & Norwich Festival and Arts Council England we created a new digital version of the project, for online audiences, which was streamed live with a range of partners throughout the UK during the summer and autumn of 2020: Battersea Arts Centre; Norfolk & Norwich Festival; Electric Dreams Festival; Traverse Theatre; AMATA at Falmouth University; Oxford Playhouse; Leicester University and HOME Manchester.

The original production was co-produced with HOME Manchester in association with Traverse Theatre Company co-commissioned by Diverse Actions, Theatre in the Mill, Norfolk & Norwich Festival, Battersea Arts Centre and Bush Theatre.

The digital production was supported by Battersea Arts Centre and Norfolk & Norwich Festival.

Both versions of the project are supported by Arts Council England

JAVAAD ALIPOOR writer, co director, performer

KIRSTY HOUSLEY co director and co-creator

PEYVAND SADEGHIAN performer

LIMBIC CINEMA projection design

JESS BERNBERG lighting

SIMON MCRORY sound

LUCY OSBORNE design

CHRIS THORPE dramaturg,

YAEL SHAVIT, creative collaborator

KAYLEIGH HAWKINS, assistant director

THE JAVAAD ALIPOOR COMPANY

www.javaadalipoor.co.uk

Prologue

PEYVAND appears as if on Instagram live: audience could watch on their mobiles. JAVAAD joins the chat.

JAVAAD

We are not the first people to feel like our world is ending.
Climate change. Pandemics. Economic collapse. The anthropocene.

PEYVAND

In Aztec myth, this world is a sterile and decrepit copy of a world
that has been seen four times before. Out of each dying world,
a new sun is born.

JAVAAD

Every society that goes through this looks back. To try and find out
what got them here. And if there is a way out.

PEYVAND

It is consumption and sacrifice that keeps the sun burning.
Human hearts. Red and pumping to keep the sun burning.
Wet and fleshy to stop the earth from cracking apart.

JAVAAD

We spend a lot of time thinking about how the world will end.
But we almost never think to ask those whose worlds have already
ended.

PEYVAND

The Aztecs knew their world was finite. And then the Spanish
arrived.

JAVAAD

This is a show about history, stories and the ending of worlds.

Scene 1 – Intro

PEYVAND

Hello, my name's Peyvand Sadeghian.

JAVAAD

And I'm Javaad Alipoor.

PEYVAND

This is a show about consumerism and digital culture.

JAVAAD

Which is why at we are going to ask be on your phones for part of this show.

There is a story that we all know, about how we came to be sat here, with these in our hands. The story is that in your hand you hold an idea dreamed up in a design studio in California that escaped into the real world, and gathered hydrocarbons from the Persian Gulf, bauxite from a mine in the Democratic Republic of Congo, parts made and assembled in Guangdong, an off-brand replacement screen fitted by a guy called Megzy in a phone shop in Luton when you broke the first one. All that rolls up and finds itself made solid in your hand. For a moment. And then it breaks.

How long have you had your phone for?

*(Audience member answers – **JAVAAD** and **PEYVAND**)*

PEYVAND

It's called built-in obsolescence. But they're not actually disposable. The thing in your hand will last in the earth for something like five million years. We evolved two hundred thousand years ago. So, our phones will last 25 times longer than we have, so far. Things like phones, plastics and microchips are what geologists have started calling techno-fossils. These are materials which have never been seen before in the sedimentary records, but are building up a layer and fusing slowly into the earth's crust. These are the kinds of geological and archeological markers that are leading to scientists to call our age the anthropece. A geological age in which human beings, anthropoi, are the defining of physical geological change.

JAVAAD

Phones do weird things to our perception of time too. If you open your calendar app and keep vigorously scrolling forward, you can be in 2244. Your phone knows it's immortal.

Part of this show will happen on your phone. Go onto Instagram, and onto our profile. It works like any other Instagram account, in that it tells you a story backwards. A normal account starts with the most recent picture and works its way back through history until 2010 when Instagram launched.

Our account tells the story of this show. We will tell you when you need to start following it. If you aren't able to follow along, look on with the person next to you as we go.

And I think its this, that's most most iconic about Instagram. The way it allows you to curate the story of your life. You use pictures to show the journey you have been on and where you come from, who you are.

PEYVAND

Throughout the show, we encourage you to use your phones and have the sound on. So if sound goes off on a video or your phone rings, don't worry, that's part of the show.

JAVAAD

The final part of Instagram we're gong to use is the "Live" function. Which is what you saw us do in our introduction. This is something you use when you want to broadcast something to your followers, supposedly as it happens. When someone goes live, they get a red line around their profile pic, so you will see one around our guy in the suit right now, and if you click on it, you can see what we are broadcasting. So you should start to hear me talking now, but also on the delay on your phone.

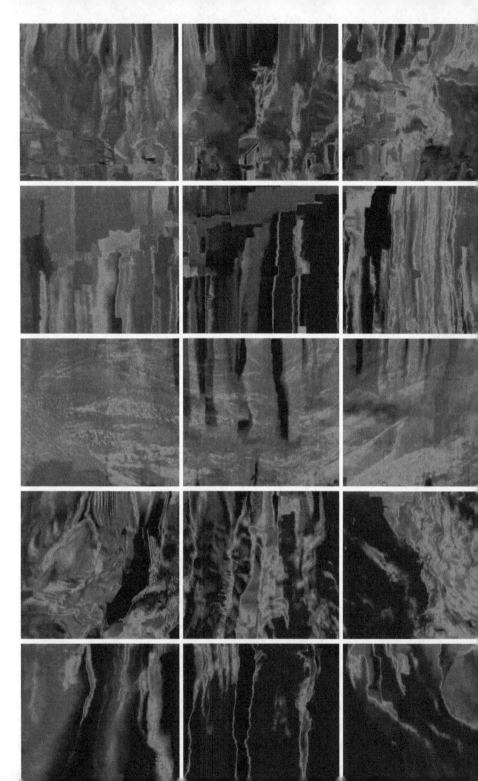

(JAVAAD films audience members on his phone)

And its on live, we're you can use all those magic augmented reality filters that we used in the introduction.

PEYVAND

Like Javaad was saying, there is something weird about calling this live. There's a delay, as the live feed arrives on your device at different times. So, effectively you get the past and the present at the same time. So going live isn't just about communicatiung from a different place. More importantly, its what you use to communicate from a different time.

JAVAAD

Now we are telling you about Instagram because it's where our story unfolds. We've been following a group of kids called "The Rich Kids of Tehran". They are a hashtag, an Instagram account and a social phenomenon.

PEYVAND

Click on the first hashtag in our profile and you'll see all the photos posted by the Rich Kids of Tehran. These are photos that other people on Instagram have posted under the Rich Kids of Tehran hashtag. So it's impossible to know why people would post such obnoxious photos of themselves, but it must be to connect themselves to something bigger and universal, cosmic even, a way of locating themselves between past and the future.

JAVAAD

They are the kids of the elite of Iranian society. Their parents sit at the intersection between the revolutionary guards, the traditional bazaar and international markets. They are a section of the men and women who overthrew the Shah, fought a ten-year war against Saddam Hussein, and pretty much most of the world, and made Islamic nationalism the household brand it is today. So I think when Iranian's see those people's children acting like this on Instagram, they feel like that history and that world is falling apart.

PEYVAND

All this came to a head at 4:49 am on April 30th 2015, when the drivers of this yellow Porsche lost control, flying from the Shariati Boulevard, a road that cuts through Niavaran, a super smart suburb in far uptown Tehran and coming to a fatal stop.

Full of drink and drugs, Hossein Rabbani Shirazi, the grandson of a famous revolutionary Ayatollah and Parivash Akbarzadeh, the middle class girl he was cheating on his fiancé with, died instantly.

JAVAAD
Their Instagram accounts went viral. People poruing over them as symbols of an increasingly out of touch elite, oblivios to the world around them, careering out of control.

PEYVAND
But its important to remember that the Rich Kids of Instagram isnt just an Iranian phenomenon. It happens all over the world. Click on that video we have put in highlights.

This is Chatunga Mugabe, Robert Mugabe's son, in a video he posted on his instagram feed, pouring a bottle of Bollinger over his Rolex, whilst sanctions in Zimbabwe are putting chicken out reach for most normal people.

JAVAAD
Obviously, people called Javaad and Peyvand are not here to tell you some story about comic black and brown people who don't know how to spend their money. There are plenty of white people up to this kind of nonsense as well.

PEYVAND
And if you'd like to look at some of these people, go back to the top of our profile and tap on the hashtag richkidsofinstagram

(Comment on pictures that appear)

JAVAAD
But this isn't a new thing and it's not just about Instagram. Rich people have always used images to display their wealth.

Three hundred years ago, Thomas Gainsborough composed this portrait of a young couple, Mr. and Mrs. Andrews, to encode details about how they had made their money, and where their economic power comes from. Now, I know what you're thinking. They both have almost exactly the same face. Let's apply Instagram's patented faceswap technology]

The two characters face's are swapped.

And, in fact we can take this experiment one step further.

(Face swap JAVAAD and PEYVAND)

But I'm not sure what this proves.

PEYVAND
It proves I look great in a pair of breeches.

JAVAAD

But the point is this. This angle on the landscape and the two tones is supposed to show how their marriage united two ones warring branches of a wealthy Westcountry land owning family.

PEYVAND

The piles of corn are indicative of the new and innovative methods of industrial farming that the thrusting Mr. Andrews is pioneering. His cocked gun tells us that there is no sweating in a mill for him, but a wealth of leisure time to hunt, play and generally bother the local badgers.

JAVAAD

Just like this traditional Safavid min-ya-toor painting encodes the different lavish hobbies of a prince, in the men at his attendance. The musician and lute imply his sponsoring of the arts. The cup of wine in his hand is a gesture towards his large cellar.

Susan Sontag pointed out that the arrival of domestic cameras in the 20th Century democratized the ability to aestheticize and record your life. Everyone could now use pictures to communicate their tastes and ambitions. We now upload more pictures to Instagram every day, than existed in total a hundred years ago.

And as the gap between the rich and poor grows to neo aristocratic levels, the new rich have made Instagram the place to stage these kinds of images.

You don't need to commission a master painter and wait eight months whilst he encodes your riches in the landscape. You can just do it yourself.

PEYVAND

In Iran this kind of Instagram life has given rise to new slang to describe these rich kids. "Aghazadeh", which is a play on the Persian word "shahzadeh", which means "princeling".

An Iranian rapper, Gdaal, had an underground hit with a tune called Aghazadeh, satirizing these kinds of kids. The image shows a picture of a 16th century princeling relaxing in the corner of a hunt or polo game. But it's photoshopped to show him wearing modern rich kids gear like a Ralph Lauren Polo and gold iPhone.

So, This is a play about the children of the international elite.

JAVAAD
It's about having all the privilege in the world and nothing but contempt for it.

PEYVAND
This is a story about the billions of tiny decisions that make up history and get us here.

JAVAAD
It's also about why you shouldn't take cocaine and drive.

PEYVAND
The feeling that you can live forever.

JAVAAD
Civilizational collapse.

PEYVAND
Thermodynamics.

JAVAAD
Instagram.

PEYVAND
Why we find it easier to imagine the end of the world than the end of humanity.

JAVAAD
The nature of narrative.

PEYVAND
What we take from the earth and what we put back into it.

JAVAAD
Rich people acting like dicks.

PEYVAND
Children fighting police and the Iranian revolution.

JAVAAD
Aztec Mythology.

PEYVAND
The half-life of Plutonium 239.

JAVAAD
Geology.

PEYVAND
Jealousy.

JAVAAD
Riding inflatable swans on rooftop swimming pools.

PEYVAND
How sedimentation develops.

JAVAAD
More cocaine.

PEYVAND
The colonial history of nuclear testing.

JAVAAD
Shopping.

PEYVAND
Astronomy.

JAVAAD
Listening to Toto's Africa in a shopping mall in Des Moines in the early 1990s.

PEYVAND

And what happens if you keep scrolling back from image to image, down through deeper and deeper layers, like a demented Instagram geologist.

JAVAAD

Go to our Instagram feed. Part One. Click on the first photo.

JAVAAD and PEYVAND cross to microphones and chairs.

PART
1

Scene 2 – Rich Kids 1

JAVAAD

4:49 am, April 30th 2015.

The Shariati Boulevard. Niavaran, far uptown in North Tehran.

This photo of a smashed-up Porsche is uploaded to Instagram and spreads across the world.

PEYVAND

Two young people were in the car, Hossein Rabbani Shirazi, from a family of famous revolutionaries, and Parivash Akbarzadeh, the middle-class girl he was cheating on his fiancé with. Hossein was a typical rich kid of Tehran, and this photo captures exactly the way poorer people see the children of the revolutionary elite. Free of the rules that everyone else has to follow. People get arrested for drinking alcohol, unmarried young men and women can't go where they please together. Obviously, this isn't anyone's actual Instagram feed. The Iranian regime tried to purge Hossein and Parivash from the internet, and when they heard about this show, the Rich Kids of Tehran threatened to sue us.

JAVAAD
Over the past few years Iran has faced increasing sanctions from the West. Especially America. But a small group of the post-revolutionary elite have found a way to bust those sanctions. The government claims everyone is fighting an economic jihad together. So the sanction-busters don't show their money in public. They don't drive yellow Porsches, but their children do and their children have Instagram, and so does everyone else.

PEYVAND
Scroll down.

4:48, one minute before the image of the crash.

Parivash is driving, swigging from a bottle of Bollinger. The car accelerates. Distance becomes pure speed. She opens the window. Sings out of it, taking off the voice of the singer they're listening to – deeper and richer than her own. The haze of champagne and declining uppers.

JAVAAD
Hossein is filming her and singing along. The road is flying past.

PEYVAND
She blows him a kiss. The steering wheel begins to pull against her hand. She grabs it.

JAVAAD
So does Hossein.

PEYVAND
She slams her foot on the brake. It feels like the car is flying away underneath them. There is no future, only now.

JAVAAD
Everything turns red.

Scroll down.

3:00 am, two hours before the crash.

Hossein and Parivash are at a party in uptown Tehran. By the gates outside the villa, a servant bribes the police. Hossein's blood boils with the hypocrisy. "Fuck them! We run this whole country" he shouts. When the lights come back on, the host tells him to leave. Hossein lunges at him. He's bundled out the door. Parivash, composes herself, she breathes out the momentary anger of having to look after him again, and checks herself in the mirror. She sits in the driver's seat and puts the key in the ignition.

Scroll down.

1:30 am, three and a half hours before the crash.

A bag of cocaine on a table. Hossein crushes, breaks, chops and racks. Rolls up notes. The cocaine glides up Khomeini's face and past the names of the martyrs. Into Hossein's network of capillaries and blood vessels and firing synapses. Music.

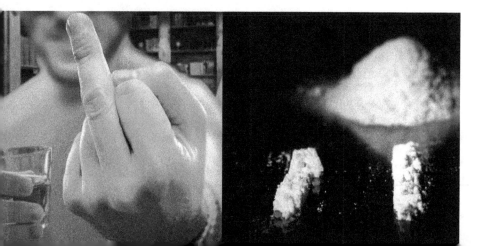

Hossein feels the cocaine pumping in his heart. A friend is teasing him, talking about war, and whether Hossein would live up to his family's reputation as soldiers. Hossein is utterly ignorant of what the question means, but then so is his friend. He says if it came to it he would kill for the revolution and his country. The friend laughs. He slaps him on the back, grabs his cheeks, "Who are you going to kill, you and all that plastic surgery?"

PEYVAND

Scroll down.

11 pm, six hours before the crash.

Parivash and Hossein arrive at the party. Shishas and bikinis. Designer dresses. A boomerang of Parivash opening a bottle of Bollinger. #Don't be jealous. #Blessings are blessings. Two months' wages in one pop of a cork. For every three glasses of Bolly or shots of Grey Goose she's offered she artfully tips two away. She's just here with one boy she has come to trust, in a way. But surrounded , with boys from the sorts of families, who can do what they want to who they want.

JAVAAD

Scroll down.

Polo shirts and swimming shorts. The international uniform of 'You can't arrest me, my dad is a lawyer'. In this country the uniform of 'You can't arrest me, my dad runs the secret police'. Parivash floats across the swimming pool on a massive inflatable swan. Hossein picks up two bottles of Bollinger and opens them. He drinks one whilst pouring the other into the swimming pool.

PEYVAND

Scroll down.

9 pm, eight hours before the crash.

Parivash is driving home from the mall, singing along to an old hit. It's syrupy and overly dramatic. The central metaphor is a mountain, but its unclear. Maybe the city is a mountain she must climb, or maybe her ambition is the mountain that nothing can conquer. Maybe him, or her love for him, is a mountain. Whatever. But this voice and this song have enveloped three generations of women. It's a frame of a kind, a perspective that makes the way the men treat them seem epic. It's not just some rubbish about the life she is going to have when she makes it uptown with her man. She knows this can't last forever and maybe tomorrow or maybe next month Hossein will get married. But right now she is alive and she feels good. In the gridlock traffic the song helps her imagine she's speeding along. Glamour and immortality will break out of the physical mountains in the north of the city. She sings along again. "You're proud, you're beautiful you don't need anyone. You are the mountains".

JAVAAD

Scroll down.

Hossein is silent. His father is holding up a newspaper and screaming at him. "Do you think you can just do what you want? You can't drive that car up and down outside the bazaar when sanctions are the way they are." Hossein wants to explode. He knows he should keep the feeling in his chest but the word rip up his rib cage and out of his throat. "I can't just sit around the house all day can I? You won't find me anything real to do". "Oh and why is that?" his dad asks, snorting, "you think you can come to work at the department? At my office? You're a disgrace." His mother plays good cop. "Now don't argue with your father. Our son can't do any old job now can he? Maybe go to Europe and do a master's degree or something." Hossein storms out. He realizes his hair is fucked and he fixes it. In the car park he throws himself across the bonnet of his Porsche and takes a photo.

PEYVAND

Scroll down.

8 hours later, that car will be flying away from underneath them. There is no future, only now.

JAVAAD

Everything turns red.

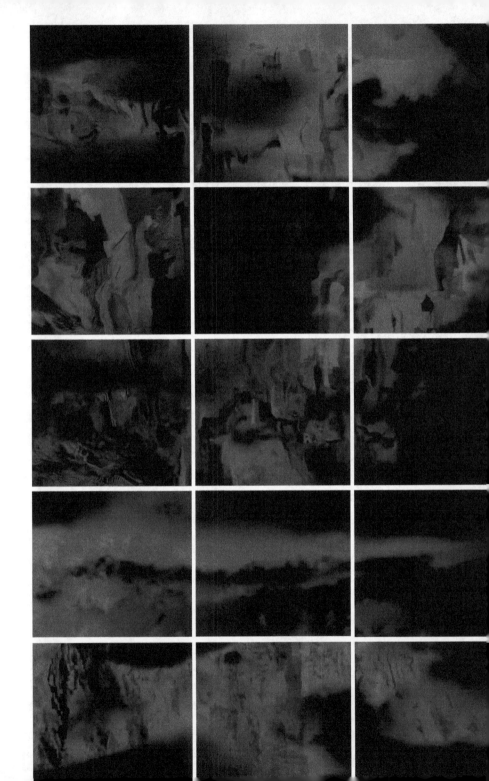

Scene 3

PEYVAND

An Instagram feed tells a story backwards over time, a story built out of discrete moments of a flow, frozen. It's always right now. The ubiquity and increasing camera power of our phones makes them able to capture smaller and smaller amounts of time for us in each image. Keeping us in ever more precise and perpetual present. When Louis Daguerre took the first ever photo with a human being in it, in 1838, it took ten minutes of exposure to capture one person. Today, taking a digital photo on a smart phone takes 16 milliseconds. People upload about 1.8 billion pictures to social media every day. Which makes 657 billion photos a year. An insane number to think of. Or to try and connect your own photos to.

JAVAAD

To put it another way, we take more photos every two minutes than existed in total in 1838. But we've always been bad at understanding certain time spans or numbers like that. Massive but finite. As human beings were good on two scales either two generations either way, or infinity; hence Muhammad, Buddha and Plato. We're especially bad at seeing ourselves in the kind of specifically fucking huge, civilizational stretches of time we need to think of to understand things like the anthropecene and climate change. It gives you this dizzying sense of history speeding up. Like Cleopatra died three times to closer to us in time, than to the founding of ancient Egypt.

PEYVAND

You dont have to go that far back or think that big to find timescales that fuck with your sense of memory. Nirvana released Nevermind closer to the release of the Beatles Sgt. Pepper than today. The release of the Beatles first LP is closer in time to the end of the First World War, than it is to us. The first iPhone was released closer in time to the fall of the Berlin wall, than it was to us.

JAVAAD

A polystyrene cup has a lifespan of over 1,000,000 years. Which is as far into the future as the invention of fire is in the past. Plutonium 239 has a half life of 24,100 years, which is as far into the future as the Chauvet cave paintings are in our past. Trying to take responsibility for a cup or nuclear waste feels impossible.

PEYVAND

This is where we begin to get into geological time. Epochs and eras. Defined by things we are laying down in the buried layers of rock. Not a register we find it easy to think of ourselves in.

JAVAAD

The parts of who we are that get captured in the rock or ice. Marks found globally.

PEYVAND

And in millions of years time people will find these traces of us, and those traces will tell the story of who we were.

JAVAAD

They'll find concrete, nuclear particles, polystyrene and plastic, and iPhones, shopping malls, air pods and polystyrene cups.

PEYVAND

And a solid layer of fossilized chicken bones that show how ten thousand years ago, we took a small bird from the Malaysian jungle, standardised and domesticated it. And how over the next five thousand years we spread them around the world.

JAVAAD

We now eat so many that we're leaving a layer of fossilizing chicken bones all around the world. In millions of years when we are all gone, ours might be called "the era of the identical clone chickens and their two-legged nemesis".

And in a way this is what's most objectively true of us as a species. The collective globalized marks we leave that are so big, that they necessitate naming a new geological era. Geologists argue about when this all started, because deciding what began the story, can help us know what we need to do stop it.

PEYVAND

The past 600 years of globalized trade are leaving marks on the earth that will be legible for millions of years. Where as the other 200,000 leave nothing. And if the whole history of the earth was put into a 24 hour clock, all of that human history would happen in the four seconds to midnight.

Scene 4 -Deep time/ Atomic bomb

("INSTAGRAM LIVE" – PEYVAND IS INSIDE THE CUBE. JAVAAD'S
COMMENTS ON APPEAR AS IF HE IS TYPING THEM.)

PEYVAND

1945. The first atomic test. Los Alamos. White men in desert heat.
Fallout particles carry across the world. A single blast changes
everything. Bones, trees, rocks, earth.

JAVAAD

Most geologists think that the anthropocene begins with the first
nuclear tests. The creation of the anthropocene begins with the
destruction of a number of worlds.

PEYVAND

Britain, America, Russia, France choose test areas. They are Black,
Brown Indigenous. In the Atlantic, Pacific and Central Asia.

JAVAAD

On an Australian island, thousands of miles from any settlement,
there is something called "the lonliest tree". Geographically, the
very furthest spot from Los Alamos. In two hundred years it will
be dead, but its bark will carry the radioactivity of that moment for
75,000 years, as it decays into earth.

All around the earth trees will become coal and oil and carry that
mark into the ground. They will become a global mark.

We talk about "human created climate change", but for the last five
hundred years "human" has meant white man".

PEYVAND

The Marshall Islands. Bikini Atoll. Evacuated Marshallese see the
sun turn purple and red. Children playing in irradiated coal.

Their genes mutating, DNA carrying the mark of what was done to
them.

Children born with no bones and translucent skin. Jellyfish babies.

JAVAAD

All humans born after 1961 have slightly radioactive teeth.

PEYVAND

Their home will be toxic for 75,000 years.

Scene 5 – Rich Kids 2

JAVAAD and PEYVAND move back to their microphones.

JAVAAD
Back to our feed. Click on Part 2. Scroll to the first photo.

Four weeks before the crash.

Hossein and Parivash arrive at the Koroush Mall. The security guards recognize him. They call him "Little Agha", he calls them "Uncle", and gives them a few notes of cash each, but they snigger about him as soon as he's passed. Him and Parivash have just got back from Dubai, and this is probably the only public place they can hang out together in Tehran , after everything that's happened.

PEYVAND
Scroll down.

They sit in the Koroush Mall and eat sushi, and take photos of themselves half-sitting half-lying on the restaurant chairs.

Scroll down.

Parivash takes a photo of herself. She plays 'too tired from all the flying and partying'. The picture shows her hand in the corner with seven shopping bags with labels in Arabic, Persian and English. She hashtags it, 'neverstopshopping'. She takes a second photo, making sure it catches the plaster on her nose, the first bit of plastic surgery her parents saved up for, and a preview of the more European nose underneath.

Scroll down.

Parivash remembers when this place opened. She didn't know Hossein then and was just like any other kid at the time – proud of this new country with bits of glamour and money, some sort of freedom. She'd daydream about actually shopping here.

As they leave, she notices an older man in the corner of the car park. He wears the uniform of a mall janitor. Two policemen are beating him. The stolen sandwiches he has hidden in his pockets squash and stain his clothes. He pleads and calls the policeman "Nephew".

Scroll down.

Parivash takes a photo of her and Hossein.

Six weeks before the crash.

Parivash sits alone in her room, in her parents' house. She sees hateful comments on her feed. People attacking her for the life she's living. Calling her classless. A downtown social climber. A slut. She thinks about the people sat thousands of miles away, scrolling down through her account and seeing a story, and is proud of it though. She's gone out and got what she wants. She deletes some of the most abusive comments. Someone has gone through every photograph and labeled each one that they think shows a new plastic surgery. But she will not turn her account off public. Never. This is her. This is a recording of how she gets to live, the places she gets to go. And if people don't like it, well its her who gets to be in it right now, and them who sit on their own wishing they could be like her.

Her sister is turning her music up loud in the room next door again. Blasting that song Aghazadeh. Trying to get under her skin. Trying to hurt her.

Scroll down.

In the corner of her room, she composes a picture. Her room is tiny. A thin window at the end of the room lets in a chink of light and the sound of sirens. Her small desk and chair are tattered, and her single bed takes up half of it. the room. But she puts a fanned-out stack of dollars on the floor. On her screen she softens the abrasive city light and makes it seem like the light of villas on the Gulf, or morning breaking over a Balearic cafe.

Her sister, Darya, bursts into the room. She throws a copy of a newspaper on the bed. The headline reads "Agahzades: a sign of corruption and social problems". She points at Hossien and his best friend on the front. "I told you. I told you, something like this would happen". Parivash says nothing, she saw the newspaper this morning. "They've taken the newspaper from the stands, but everyone saw it this morning" Darya says. "Dad's gone mental." Parivash can't believe her sister would go out of her way to show him. Darya reads this on her face "I didn't even tell him. The whole neighbourhood is talking about you. You're not going anywhere".

Scroll down.

Hossein is in the car outside, but her dad is in the corner of the room, his belt in his hand. Parivash looks down at her phone as it rings. He slaps it out of her hand. She picks it up and runs outside. She gets in the car and breathes out. Hossein grabs her hand, and asks her how she is doing. Makes everything easy. On the side of the street a young man is waiting for a cop to pass. When he leaves he takes a spray can and writes on the wall. "#the hungry ones are coming".

The drab middle class districts and the slums downtown fall away from her, Hossein accelerates and she takes off into the neon pink and artificial purples.

JAVAAD
Scroll down.

Six weeks and one day before the crash

Hossein sits in the small guest room of his father's offices. His dad had promised to get him something decent to do at the ministry, but he's fucked it up again. He just needs a chance to show what he's capable of. At times like this he gets this nagging feeling of self hatred. It starts off like a voice in his ear and then becomes something physical that crawls up and down the inside of his skin. His dad's assistant comes back into the room. Hossein can see the flicker of contempt in the old man' smile. "Little agha" he says "boy king", feigning subserviance "your father wants me to tell you that now might not be the right time for you to start on a public life." Hossein swallows it down. "Can't I talk to my dad". "No, he will see you at home." Hossein goes to storm out the door and the little old man grabs him his hand. Boney fingers cut into his writsts. "If you are going to run around with whores, try not to get caught," he hisses in Hossein's ear.

So when the old man leaves, he sits here and pulls out the flask of expensive smuggled in brandy he carries and racks a line of coke on a portrait of the Supreme Leader. "Fuck them," Hossein thinks. "The world is full of hate and jealousy. They want to have my life and watch it, but they can't bear that I actually live it". He sends Parivash a text. Tells her he wants to go to Dubai again.

Scroll down.

He does another shot. Films it. Flips a gesture at the camera. When he puts it on Instagram, he doesn't realize that his followers will soon recognize his father's office. And the scandal will get deeper for him and his family.

Scene 6 – Shopping Malls

JAVAAD

Tehran is like any other city – you can find out everything you need to know about it from the history of its shopping malls. Koroush Mall, The kind of shopping mall that Hossein and Parivash might hang out in, are in the far north of the city. Over the past two decades the richest suburbs of the city have moved further and further North, into the mountains where the filth and the smog of downtown can't travel. The capital for the shopping centres put up by men like Hossein's father – who use their connections to the international markets, and political connections in Iran to get permits to import the newest Western brands.

(Projection of Tehran shopping malls map.)

PEYVAND

Koroush Mall is named after the indigenous Persian pronunciation of Cyrus, as in Cyrus the Great. He's the mythologized founder of the first Persian Empire. He's been a symbol of Iranian nationalism for about two hundred years, for the monarchists, and the Islamic Republic. You'll definitely know him from his substantial donations to the British Museum. So, there's four thousand years of history in the plastic decorations by the main entrance. The same brands you might find in Dubai or West London.

JAVAAD

If you scroll down further into the past, and twenty kilometres
South, you reach where uptown was fifty years ago. Here the Shah
built the Plasco Centre as a symbol of his regime's modernizations.
Keep scrolling further South and you meet the Grand Bazaar.
A building sprawling ten kilometres in every direction. For four
hundred years it was the centre of the city.

PEYVAND

Scroll down even further to the far South of the city, and you can
follow the five-thousand-year journey of the city back down to the
ancient Neolithic settlement in a poorer suburb today called Reyy.

JAVAAD

These are some of the oldest remains of human settlement. Like
others in the Middle East, Africa and China they show market
places and areas for trading. Buildings for maintaining an economic
surplus. It's in these that we learn the basic story............ about how
our world developed......

PEYVAND

And the way we look at those remains now to tell us about who
we were then, our shopping centres will be looked at in the future.

They are made out of concrete, so like Roman remains they will last for hundreds of thousands of years. You can even think of them as geological markers of our age. Geologists define markers as things that are globally present and leave sedimentary foundations. Shopping malls are globally present, with the same shops everywhere, and their physical foundations are a layer of concrete sediment.

Geologists also talk about how the fossil record of this moment will show a collapse of global diversity, but at the same time much more diversity in every given location. Like being able to get any kind of food, but from only from the same chains, in any mall in the world.

Scene 7 – Deep time/ Oil and Coal

*Broadcast through Instagram – **PEYVAND** Going Live. **JAVAAD**
comments on the live footage through text comments.*

JAVAAD

Some argue that the Anthropocene begins with the extraction of oil.
And the destruction of the Muslim worlds of the Middle East.

PEYVAND

One layer further down. In the Persian Gulf, three miles beneath the
sea bed there is a hole where the past should be. On the shore a
tall thin white man, just arrived from the British Petroleum company.
He looks out to sea. Smoky, warping desert air. Dirty Red Sun.

JAVAAD

The Industrrial revolution has left a spike in carbon dioxide , its
physical effect , frozen into the Antarctic ice cores, the bark of
trees, limestone, fossilised bones and shells.

PEYVAND

The villagers are unaware of the machine guns being set up. They
don't see the cars as they arrive. Bullets fly through the air. Women
and children and men run towards the shore.

The village is cleared. Messages from London. Marshlands are drained.

JAVAAD

All energy on the earth comes from the sun. Oil and coal are
deposits of the unused energy of the past trapped under the
ground.

PEYVAND

When the night comes the villages have been taken. More company
men arrive. Maps and plans are drawn up. It was clear, and full of
God's gifts and pearls. The rivers dry and the sea turns black.

JAVAAD

Huge machines sit in the middle of the sea. We draw the past up
into the present, and we burn it to accelerate into the future.

PART

3

Scene 8 – Rich Kids

PEYVAND
Part three

Scroll down.

One year before the crash.

When the plane touches down in Dubai, Parivash squeezes Hossein's hand. This is her first time outside of Iran, she hasn't slept at all.

JAVAAD
Hossein wakes up slowly. As he stirs he knocks his knees into the drink holder. He's use to first class but kind of snuck here with Parivash. Just put it on the credit card and didn't tell his parents.

PEYVAND
Scroll down.

The hotel room is huge. Parivash takes a photo of the city skyline- her manicured hand just visible in the corner. This is it. She thinks. She opens up her phone and video calls her sister... She asks if Mum and Dad have gone to bed and Darya tells her that they have. She shows Darya the room, and Darya can't believe that she isn't using a filter. Parivash asks Darya whether the lie she's told her parents is holding, and Darya says that it is. Parivash makes Darya promise to message her if her parents suspect anything.

She hangs up and walks downstairs. The valet walks her to the hire car, and the automatic door of the rented yellow ferrari pops open. She offers Hossein a swig of champagne.

Scroll down.

JAVAAD

Wagyu and Oysters and more champagne at the 27th floor place at burj al arab.

At dinner Hossein is showing off his knowledge of the city. How much he's been here before. He tells Parivash the story of the city, how it emerged almost fully formed from the desert.

Scroll down.

That night, as they drive by the waterfront, Hossein points to the hotels and bars as they fly past. Moorish souks, Byzantine palaces, Persian gardens. Dubai: The Las Vegas of the Middle East. A pastiche of thousands of years history glimmer around them conjured from glass, chrome and plastic. The long generations of the dead, returning eternally to party.

Scroll down.

The next morning they eat breakfast hungover. Hossein wants to go back to bed but Parivash wants to drive out of the city.

PEYVAND

Scroll down.

Three diet cokes and four paracetamol each later they are driving out to AL Bastikiyya, the old Persian quarter. Parivash read about it before they came – something about it, the only preserved bit of the local culture, maybe the way it was built by Iranians fleeing religious persecution centuries ago, or maybe the weird way that its preserved as ancient amidst all the brand new "architecture" made her want to see it.

JAVAAD

Hossein scrolls through his phone in the passenger seat.

PEYVAND

Scroll down.

When they arrive at the old Persian quarter it's nearly noon so the streets are deserted. The air is thin and burning hot. Parivash has to almost drag Hossein from the car.

In the central square Parivash takes the scene in. An old woman is beating the dust from a carpet against the side of the road. The sun warms yellows from the bricks of the ancient outer walls of the surrounding houses.

JAVAAD

Hossein takes a drink from the fountain in the square. He walks over to the Parivash.

PEYVAND

Parivash has a heart full of stuff she wants to say. She wants to tell Hossein that the old woman makes her think of how quickly history moves – how a generation ago, both of their families would live like this, in a part of Tehran that had slowness and chador wearing women and extended families sharing rooms like this. That the class difference between them is less than sixty years old. That she doesn't care that he won't leave his fiancé and that even if her father finds out, and even if her mother knows she wouldn't really care because she will only ever be being passed from one man to another, however much she studies. From her father's house to her husband's. That to carve out a moment when you feel alive is worth an eternity of flowing along.

JAVAAD

They sit next to each other, on the side of the fountain. Hossein lights a cigarette. Hossein knows she's deep in thought. Something about the old woman moves him too.

PEYVAND

Parivash takes a drag on his cigarette. "In a way," she says, "It's better if you're silent sometimes." "like a mountain, like in the old song you know". "silent or patient like a mountain, or we drive up the mountain together and just stop all the normal boring chatter of life or whatever. The point is we're having fun and nothing lasts forever."

JAVAAD

"Mountains last forever don't they?" Hossein asks

PEYVAND

Parivash looks at him "They erode, you idiot".

JAVAAD

They sit silently together in the heat. The rhythmic beating of the woman's beater on the carpet. Things that they will never know how to begin to say to each other. Hossein takes out his phone – he shrugs off the weird feeling by scrolling up and down his instagram profile. The heat is intense. There is just silence. Things they cannot say. And that echoing banging cutting through and rattling the heat. It fills up Hossein's head and begins to get inside him as he scrolls.

PEYVAND

Parivash is struggling to focus on her phone screen. Scrolling to try and let go of the feeling. That banging rattling around in her skull, feeling like it's dragging her back to it.

Scroll down.

They both begin to feel sick and woozy and suddenly, it's like they are falling backwards.

Pictures flash past them. Some are from twenty years ago. The first pair of western trainers his father managed to get for him. The war had just ended, and his father promised to get him some Nike's, but all he managed to get was Gola, for god's sake. Nineties though. Actually, they're coming back.

JAVAAD

But that's not important now. They fall faster and deeper into the screen and further and further down the time line. They see pictures they only vaguely recognize. Hossein as a child by the grand Bazaar. Tehran just beginning to be rebuilt. Hossein's father in military fatigues. The war with Iraq. The revolution. What the actual fuck.

PEYVAND

Mushroom clouds break through. The arrival of the British and the Portuguese in the Persian Gulf, war ships on the horizon. Steam engines and the cracking of rock, and the pickaxe handle drives him further down. All at once it disappears and everything turns black.

JAVAAD

Hossien and Parivash can hardly see anything through black. They are floating through what seems like deep space. As Hossein's eyes adjust, he makes out the feint glimmers of light breaking through around him. The lights are like neon figures that he half recognizes from school text books. Ancient Persian and Greek Kings. Stone Age Warriors. Medieval Shahs and early British Imperialists. It's not deep space he is floating in, but deep time. One of the figures begins to get closer and closer. Hossein panics and turns to Parivash but she is further away into the void. The figure is towering above him and pops into three weirdly Instagram photoshopped dimensions. Hossein recognises him from a documentary or a record cover or something. He's dressed almost like a 14th century nobleman. A young prince. Almost entirely 14th century apart from the purple Ralph Laruen polo shirt he's wearing and the gold I phone in his hand. Hossein's eyes fill with terror and confusion. Eyes fixed on the incongruity of the mobile device.

PEYVAND

"Great, isn't it," The timeless princeling says "Got it here actually, we have like this super weird atemporal version of The Cyrus Mall we have here. I mean it's real gold. Cool no?"

JAVAAD

"What are you?" Hossein asks.

PEYVAND

"Oh yeah sorry, totally, sorry. I am Prince Tahmasp Isma-eel Jah-an-gir Seyf-al-Dow-lah."

JAVAAD

Hossein looks on blankly.

PEYVAND

"I'm basically the youngest son of some ancient king you've never heard of. Never heard of cos I never really did anything. I've been here for five hundred years bro. Just kind of floating around. But its cool bro, we have malls here, and there is like a really cool sushi place."

JAVAAD

Hossein sees Parivash far away, but can see that she is looking at the prince too. "Why have you brought me here?" he asks.

PEYVAND

"Oh I didn't bring you here bro," says the prince. It's where you belong. This is the place where you end up if you were playing polo and hunting while the British arrived in the Gulf and the Russians arrived in the Caspian. Being dead for six hundred years gives you a certain perspective, bro. You need to get a handle on things."

JAVAAD

When they come to by the fountain, they walk silently back to the car. Hussain shakes off the vision and puts the key in the ignition.

Scene 9 – Mallwave

JAVAAD

As older millennials, we are on the older side of people who use these platforms.

PEYVAND

For the Instagram native generation, it's a much more creative thing. They shape reality with it. Imagining and photoshopping whole worlds that may or may not have actually existed.

JAVAAD

One interesting example of this is an online movement called "vaporwave". Its named after vaporware, the name that software engineers give to software that was never completed or reached the market. By extension, vaporwave is sound and music and images made out of the recycled parts of retro-software and bits of the Internet. Like this piece of music, which has bits of Windows 95, Windows XP. Old Geocities websites. .... Vaporwave music and visuals are a ghost made out of bits of a past that never quite was.

PEYVAND

One recent subgenre of vaporwave is called mallwave. Go back to our profile and click on hashtag mallwave.

Beat

This hashtag orders all of the images tagged with Mallwave. There are millions on Insta and more on Youtube. ....

It's about the feeling of hyper-abundance in the late Reagan to early Clinton eras. It's put together by 15-year old stoners in the US, or kids who are just fans of the kind of 90s teen comedy that revolves around a shopping mall. Over the past few years, shopping malls and high streets have collapsed. This is a celebration of the bits they left behind.

JAVAAD

This is one of the biggest mallwave videos, two and a half million views. It's the loop of Toto's Africa playing over empty shopping malls. It's the smell of pretzels. It's the feeling of going to a mall in a fairly bleak part of small-town America and getting swamped in something warm and fuzzy. Saved by the Bell, shopping, lip gloss, Buffy the Vampire Slayer, Stranger Things. The soft tinkle of the sound of fountains and the warm synths of the music coming from hidden speakers.

PEYVAND

The hashtag 'mallwave' has a few million followers on Instagram. Mallwave might be easier to understand if those kids were our age, in that they we remember retail high street shopping, and a time before Amazon. But it isn't. It's mainly for younger people, eighteen and nineteen-year olds who don't remember a time before the great recession or the rise of internet consumerism.
If you talk to them online or read their comments everyone circles around the same thing. An awareness that this isn't the same kind of way that you might consume regular pop music or culture.

JAVAAD

It's something used to unplug and relax to. It's a sort of creative way of digging up the past and finding the last heroic age of consumer capitalism, the last time, they are told, when it felt like life was getting better, bit by bit. To remind them, as one kid said, of a time they never knew, when things weren't quite as shitty.

Scene 10 – Rich Kids 4

JAVAAD

2010, Five years before the crash.

Instagram is yet to reach Iran and Hossein and Parivash are yet to meet. Hossein's father is a fat old man sitting at the height of power. Links to the Revolutionary Guards, the bazaar and the international markets. He is about to sink his money into a new shopping complex; The Cyrus Shopping Mall. To understand Hossein and Parivash's story, how they met their end in that crash, we have to go deeper into the past, into a time when people fought revolutions and built and betrayed countries. Back before Instagram existed, when stories were made of stuff more cinematic and sepia.

PEYVAND

1985, Thirty years before the crash. The height of the Iran Iraq war.

Hossein's father crouches in the back of a truck crossing the border into Kurdish Iraq. A man is tied up next to him. One hundred miles inside the border and the truck stops.

The Americans are wearing Kurdish clothes. They speak American accented Kurdish and Persian. They promise 500 anti-tank missiles, but the Revolutionary Guards are to use their sway to have American hostages freed in Lebanon. They want a guarantee.

Hossein's father walks back to the truck. The tied-up man is writhing. Hossein's father grabs at him to keep him still. He leans in close and threatens him. Takes off his hood; the man bites him hard. A blow and the man is silent.

Hossein's father heaves the man up on to his shoulder and walks back. He throws him in front of the Americans. The Americans immediately recognise the man as a member of the rival faction of the Revolutionary Guards. "You boys sure know how to make an impression," one American says. Hossein's father replies in heavily accented English: "We know how to make you take us seriously".

December 1971, 44 years before the crash.

Eight years, and a whole world before the Iranian revolution. Hossein's father is one of hundreds of thousands of poor kids in traditional families, watching the height of the Shah's pomp, on small TVs in the corner of small two room homes.

In the desert sun, picked out slightly too red by the cameras, he sees the Shah. The TV announcer gives the date in the new calendar year the Shah has forced on the country, and the titles he has taken from Cyrus the Great. King of Kings, Shadow of God on Earth.

In the desert the sun breaks from behind a cloud. The Shah steps forward.

Video of the shah

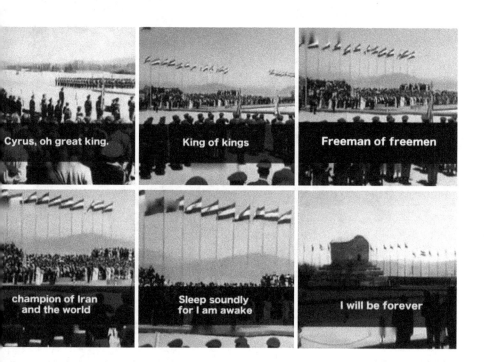

When he arrives at his father's stall in the bazaar, Hossein's father sneaks for a cigarette with Morteza, who works on the stall next door.

Every cinema in Tehran will be showing the film of that morning's speech tonight. Morteza has never seen Hossein's father like this. His eyes are clear and he holds his body straight. He invites Morteza to join him and some of the other young bazaaris after evening prayers.

When Morteza arrives, Hossein's father is already splitting the boys up into look-outs and window breakers. By 3am there isn't a single cinema window left unsmashed in the surrounds of the bazaar, or a poster left up.

As they stand triumphant under the final window Morteza scrawls "Death to the King, death to America" on the wall.

A whistle. Two policemen are running towards them. The boys begin to scatter. Hossein's father remains rooted to the spot. As the first policeman gets closer, he feels the knife in his pocket. The policeman goes down.

In the darkness his colleague sees him hit the floor and stops running. He begins to blow his whistle harder. More will arrive soon.

As Hossein's father runs home, he feels like a freedom fighter. Like a jihadi. In his mind, in this dream that returns throughout his life, he'll never stop running.

Through being the hero of the bazaar to being the hero of the streets and the Revolutionary Guard. To toppling this King of Kings, fighting in a bloody desert and trech war, and then building a new state. He'll keep on running further up town, to opportunity and wealth, and a family and a son, that he never really understands, and who never really knows where he came from.

Scene 11 – Entropy

(PEYVAND and JAVAAD in front of first projector screen.)

PEYVAND

There is no such thing as time. No past. No future. There's no reason why time as we feel it should be a physical thing.

JAVAAD

We just think of it as being linear because effect always seems to follow cause. Time can't be reversed. We can't actually go backwards.

PEYVAND

But the difference between past and future, between cause and effect, between memory and hope, between regret and intention.... In the elementary laws that describe the mechanisms of the universe, there is no such difference.

Forward in time is just the direction in which we gain knowledge and entropy increases.

JAVAAD

Entropy is the measure of how disordered a system is. Everything in the universe moves from a more ordered state and begins to fall apart. In any physical activity, if you turn on a light, or try and power an electrical circuit, you lose some of your ordered energy as heat.

PEYVAND

The ultimate end of everything is the heat death of the universe. All order gone into a sort of homogenous custard of matter of the same temperature.

JAVAAD

Time emerges because we are the kind of animals who look for order and narrative in things. Time is basically a measure of to what extent things are falling apart.

PEYVAND

In the 1930s Walter Benjamin described looking at this painting by Paul Klee: Angelus Noves.

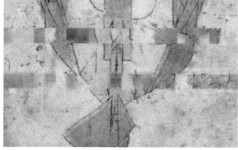

JAVAAD

Benjamin thinks this is what the angel of history would look like. His eyes and mouth open, wings outstretched, face turned towards the past. "Where we see the appearance of a chain of events, he sees one single catastrophe, which unceasingly piles rubble on top of rubble and hurls it before his feet."

PEYVAND

He wants to pause for a moment to awaken the dead and piece together what has been smashed, but he can't. The storm that is blowing from paradise is so strong that he can't close his wings, so it blows him irresistibly into the future, and around him the rubble heap and corpses keep growing.

JAVAAD

This storm is what we call progress.

Scene 12 – Deep Time / Orbis Spike

BROADCAST THROUGH INSTAGRAM – PEYVAND GOING LIVE. JAVAAD
COMMENTS ON THE LIVE FOOTAGE THROUGH TEXT COMMENTS.

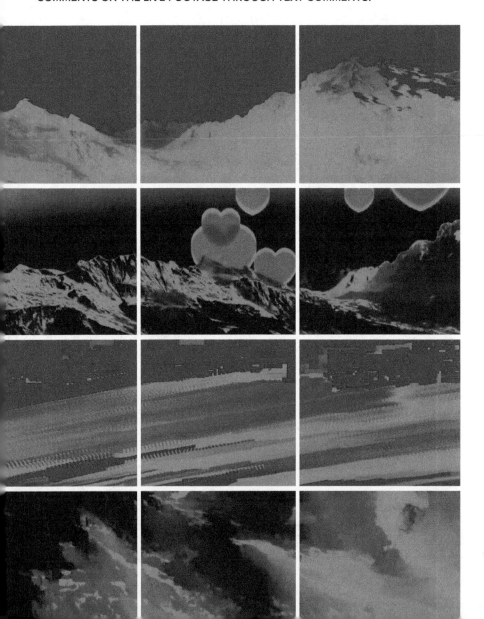

PEYVAND

Dawn. A Mexican beach. The Aztec Empire is crumbling. The sun picks yellows and greens from blue water. Blacks and browns from the Spanish galleons on the horizon.

JAVAAD

The oldest trace of the anthropocene is a mark left from the dawn of colonialism and capitalism. It lies far under the Antarctic ice. Europeans killed 50 million indigenous Americans. 50 million fewer people exhaling carbon dioxide. So many people died and so much land went wild that the global drop in CO_2 output left a mark in the Antarctic ice core. This mark is called the Orbis Spike.

PEYVAND

Spanish disease and murder have already spread through the Aztec empire. The woman knows the Spanish are coming for her nation next.

Cities are empty. Temples overgrown. The red flag of victory and Christ the Redeemer.

She could die here. Or in battle. Of starvation, or in a band that resisted the Spanish. Smallpox, or the flu, or any other European disease. A final gasp of bloody choking.

JAVAAD

The invasion of the Americas, the slave trade and colonialism that followed led to an unprecedented transfer of commodities and species. This is called the columbian exchange.

PEYVAND

As her final breath leaves her mouth it floats upwards towards the sky, and coheres with 50 million others. Blown south by the wind. Trapped under the antarctic ice.

She will stare up from the ice for five hundred years. See those who extract, and mine, and claim above her. The sun turning purple.

JAVAAD

We talk about "human created climate change", but for the last five hundred years "human" has meant white man".

There isn't an Anthropocene that connects us. There is a scar that divides. The Orbis spike and the columbian exchange were done by some people to some others.

PEYVAND

Bodies made extractable. Wet and fleshy earth.

Finally, in the ice at the core of the Arctic there is a layer of sedimentation, The Orbis Spike, an image of history that we cannot delete. Sometimes I think about finding that one woman's last gasp and freeing it, taking it back five hundred years onto that deathbed she was left on, and just cupping it and putting it back through her mouth to her lungs. And taking her back. Even beyond that moment. I'd stand with her on the beach as the sun picked yellows and greens out of the blue water, and blacks and browns where the Spanish galleons get closer. And she would whisper to me that there will never be a thing called the Anthropocene because there isn't an Anthropos. Not here. There are two people, a woman on a beach waiting for the end to arrive, and a white man looking back at her, about to bring it.

JAVAAD

Which is why 50 million being killed in the Americas is only the beginning. There is a world to be colonized.

PEYVAND

So property, commerce, patriarchy that began in the Neolithic will accelerate and mutate.

JAVAAD

Four-fifths of the world and its people become property to be harvested.

PEYVAND

West Africa and India will become the biggest prizes to be taken.

JAVAAD

So Europeans will need to find new ways of powering their ships, and new places to moor them on the routes to India.

PEYVAND

So modernity arrives, on the competing gunships of the Portuguese and the Russians and the British, in places like Iran.

JAVAAD

And traditional life is smashed apart, and people lose the ability to support themselves from land. So that all of history and commerce can be made to flow through Europe.

PEYVAND

So when the industrial revolution hits its stride, the Middle East will already be in freefall, and Iranian oil fields will be claimed by the British Petroleum company.

JAVAAD

So a man will be sent from London to organize the expulsion of the people who live on the oil fields. And the Iranian Shahs will become puppets of the West.

PEYVAND

And generations will dream of freeing their countries.

JAVAAD

And the West will dream of bigger and better empires, so that the great powers will need apocalyptic new bombs.

PEYVAND

So islands and deserts are cleared for bombs to be tested. Tribes driven across the sea.

JAVAAD

Every human being born since 1961 is born with slightly radioactive teeth.

PEYVAND

And in Iran people will dream of freedom and owning their own oil, but the Americans will bring the final Shah to power. So he will feel like a puppet.

JAVAAD

So he will build places like the Plasco Shopping Centre to show he is modern.

PEYVAND

And one morning in the desert he will claim to stand in the immortal line of Cyrus the Great.

JAVAAD

So men like Hossein's father, whose world has crumbled, will be driven further away from him, and they will overthrow his regime.

PEYVAND

Which will mean that the longest trench war of human history will be fought over the control of the bodies and earth of the Iranian oil fields.

JAVAAD

So men like Hossein's father will have to learn to break international sanctions to bring weapons to the country.

PEYVAND

Which means that when the war ends and Hossein's father goes back to civilian life, his links to the bazaar and international trade place him to bring postmodern consumerism to Iran.

JAVAAD

So in Tehran he will commission a jumbled version of all this history, built out of plastic and concrete, and call it the Koroush Mall.

PEYVAND

So when Hossein grows up with money, and meets a girl called Parivash, they will both search in that jumble of history for something they can get some sort of traction on. But there'll be nothing to do but go to Dubai or take her shopping to the Koroush shopping mall, and they can briefly be people to aspire to or dream of being.

JAVAAD

But that means that when the sanctions bite again and the economy collapses, Hossein and Parivash will become typical examples of the rich kids of Tehran that more and more people hate.

PEYVAND

Which makes Hossein feel trapped between a vision of being some kind of heir to his father's regime, and also an heir to his money.

JAVAAD

And of course, Hossein can't understand this, and Parivash won't give up her taste of a kind of freedom, which means when he storms out of his parents' house they drive to a party uptown.

PEYVAND

And with all that, and the drugs and the booze in his head, at 3am in the morning Hossein throws himself at the host.

JAVAAD

Which means when they are thrown out of the party, they have nothing to do but finish their coke and Bolly and race his new yellow Porsche up and down the Shariati Boulevard, blasting tunes. Which means at 4:48 am Parivash loses control.

PEYVAND

And everything turns red.

Scene 13 – Göbekli Tepe

PEYVAND

Everywhere, people feel like things are ending: economies, ecologies, political systems, civilisations.

JAVAAD

If we want to know how to change direction, we have to know where we started from. Or there really is nothing else to do but put your foot down and accelerate.

PEYVAND

1995. A grassy plain somewhere between Turkey, Iraq and Iran. A team of archeologists and geologists make a discovery that upends how we think of human history.

JAVAAD

At Göbekli Tepe, they found a huge stone temple with evidence of early beer brewing. It was built around 14,000 years ago. Kilometers in length. Carved with vivid images of animals and humans. The whole complex points towards Sirius, the dog star.

PEYVAND

The discovery of Göbekli Tepe was a challenge to the 200-year-old paradigm of how human societies began. For hundreds of years European archeologists had a rigid story about human development. Commerce before culture. Market place before temples. Farming before beer brewing. But history isn't linear. It turns out we were artists, star gazers and vintners before we had 'so called' civilization.

JAVAAD

The discovery of Gobekli Tepe fundamentally changes the story of human development.

Imagine the people and society that built Stonehenge. That was 4,000 years ago. Gobekli Tepe had already been buried for 9,000 years.

The 200,000 years of human prehistory before the story we all know, are not full of darkness and nothing. Commerce didn't come first, trying to make sense of the things around us did. Göbekli Tepe stood for four thousand years, which is ten times as long as the Houses of Parliament has stood. And then for some reason it was meticulously and carefully buried at the dawn of the Neolithic, sitting undisturbed for 13,000 years before it was found under that hill in Iran, Iraq, and Turkey in 1995.

PEYVAND

It's almost impossible to know what the social function of Göbekli Tepe was, but it must have been a way for them to see themselves in relation to something universal and cosmic. A way of locating themselves between past and future.

JAVAAD

When we were researching this show, we spoke to a geologist, and she told us that they think about the earth like a hard drive or a computer server, a store of information and past decisions. Everything we've ever done, and everything we've ever been, left in the earth. The earth is full of stories about who we are, and one of them says that before we did anything else, we would gather twice a year to get drunk and wonder about the stars.

PEYVAND

We've deleted the feed you've been following: Some things we dig up and some things we bury.

Printed in the USA
CPSIA information can be obtained
at www.ICGtesting.com
JSHW012013140824
68134JS00024B/2396